From GOD tc

The Icon's Journey to Your Heart

John Kosmas Skinas

Ancient Faith Publishing • Chesterton, Indiana

From God . . . to You

Here you are, before the sacred gates, about to enter into the mystery of the icons. God has given them to you so you can see that heaven is always just a prayer away. Burned, smashed, and buried, icons have endured a great deal as they've made their way from God to you. They've reached you because He wants them in your church, in your home, and in your hands. But most of all, God wants you to keep His image in your heart, where, if you listen closely, you can hear His message with every beat: "I am with you always, even until the end of time" (Matthew 28:20).

Holy Virgin Cathedral—Joy of All Who Sorrow, San Francisco, California

Sealed with His Image

The story of how God sent the very first icon to us goes like this: Long ago, in the time of Jesus, lived a dying king. His name was Abgar, and leprosy was eating away his life. Desperate and scared, King Abgar sent a messenger to beg Jesus to come a long distance to save him. Instead, Jesus pressed His face into a cloth and gave it to the messenger, who hurried back to Abgar. The king unfolded the cloth and found an image of Christ looking back at him. This is how Jesus went to heal the scared king: through an icon. So when you're feeling scared or helpless, turn to Jesus. Remember that when you were baptized, your very heart, like Abgar's cloth, was sealed with Christ's image, making you more royal than any earthly king could ever be.

NOTICE THIS →

We can learn much from just the face of Jesus. His eyes are firm yet loving. He has used His ears to hear His Father's will so that He might obey. And His mouth is small, reminding us that we should only speak when our words will make God happy.

The Icon Not Made by Hands

Also called "The Holy Napkin" or "The Holy Face"

God with Us

"The Lord will give you a sign: the Virgin shall bear a Son; you shall call His name Emmanuel, God with us." Every icon ever made is a joyful picture of these words from the Prophet Isaiah about Jesus. This is so because every icon calls out, "God is with us." He's not only all around us; He's inside of us. He knows what we're thinking before we even think it! So if you're feeling sad, distracted, or angry—tell Jesus. If you don't even feel like praying—tell Him. Ask Him to set your heart right. Icons remind us that God is always reaching out to us. Sometimes we take hold of His hand, and sometimes we push it away. Mary took hold of God's hand and never let go. Her example, along with those of the saints, helps us live St. Paul's words: "It is no longer I who live, but Christ who lives in me" (Galatians 2:20).

NOTICE THIS →

How many circles can you find in this icon? Circles are the symbol of perfection and eternity. The one behind Jesus is dotted with stars, showing us that the Virgin Mary holds the Maker of the Universe inside her body.

Virgin of the Sign

Gifts

God gives us wheat and grapes. We turn them into bread and wine and give them back to Him. He then turns the bread and wine into the ultimate gift: Holy Communion. A similar transformation of gifts takes place when iconographers—with wood and paint—create icons, which then become fountains of God's grace and joy. St. Luke, the first of Christ's followers to become an iconographer, learned much about Jesus by becoming His mother's friend. Tradition tells us that Mary not only shared her memories of Jesus with Luke, but even gave him her wooden kitchen table to make into an icon! From God to Mary to Luke to us—gifts of love are always in motion, passed from person to person. A gift can be as simple as smiling at someone who needs cheering up. Gifts like this are then passed to others, bringing a little more of heaven down to earth.

NOTICE THIS →

It's no accident that the image of St. Luke painting his icon looks so much like the one of him writing his Gospel. Icons and the Bible are different forms of the same truth. Instead of letters, icons use color and shapes to reveal God's Word.

Saint Luke Painting the First Icon

The Lamp of the Body

The Church learned much about creating icons from the ancient Egyptians, Greeks, and Romans. The early Christians of Egypt created a special style of iconography that lives on today. In the icon here, Mary and Joseph have been painted with large heads and radiant faces to show that they're full of prayer. Saints in Egyptian icons also have widened eyes, which look beyond this world to the realities of heaven. They appear almost childlike, reflecting how kids like you are icons of purity. Hold on to your innocence! When you're tempted to look at bad images on a screen or on a page, turn to the holy images. "The lamp of the body is the eye. If therefore your eye is good, your whole body will be full of light" (Matthew 6:22–23).

NOTICE THIS →

An angel has come down from heaven, fish have swum to the surface of the water, and birds have flown down from the sky; the creatures of heaven and earth gather around Jesus, the Source of Life, as He passes by.

Flight into Egypt

The Fountain of Life

Life wasn't easy for the early Christians. Their enemies wanted to destroy them and their faith. So they had to worship secretly in the catacombs, the underground cemeteries found throughout the Roman Empire. To keep the church hidden and safe, early Christians often used symbols instead of icons when decorating the walls of the catacombs.

Only other Christians could understand the symbols' secret language. Jesus was shown as a lamb, fish, or young shepherd. The peacock, which ancient people believed drank from the "fountain of life" and could live forever, also became a symbol for Jesus. These catacomb images were painted prayers and expressions of hope that helped the early Church remember Christ's words: "Do not be afraid; I am the First and the Last. I am He Who Lives, and was dead, and behold, I am alive forevermore" (Revelation 1:17–18).

NOTICE THIS →

When these royal gates are closed, the shapes under the peacocks' beaks form a chalice. The communion chalice is the true "fountain of life." Jesus said that whoever drinks from it will live forever.

Royal Gates in the Form of Peacocks
Holy Trinity Greek Orthodox Church, San Francisco, California

The Word Became Flesh

Once it became safe to be a Christian, icons were brought from their hiding places into the new churches that were springing up across the Roman Empire. Some showed Jesus as a triumphant king with long hair; others presented Him as a beardless young shepherd with short hair. The church decided that the best way to show the grown-up Jesus is the way He appeared to King Abgar on the Holy Napkin: with long brown hair and a beard. One of the oldest of these icons can be found at St. Katherine's Monastery in the Sinai Desert of Egypt. Around one thousand five hundred years old, this icon celebrates the fact that "the Word became flesh and dwelt among us" (John 1:14). Christ's two upright fingers remind us that He is both fully God and fully human. They are slightly bent to show that God came down from heaven for us. The three fingers that touch each other symbolize the Holy Trinity. Jesus is blessing you in the name of the Father, Son, and Holy Spirit, reminding you to use your own hands for works of love and kindness.

NOTICE THIS →

Try covering half of Jesus' face with your hand. Now cover the other half. The stern side reminds us how we need to live the Gospel. The gentle, blessing side reminds us that He loves us even when we fail to do this.

Christ
Pantocrator
Also called
“Sinai Christ”

Eyes on God

Even though the church settled on the best ways to show Jesus, He doesn't always look the same in every icon. We need to remember that an icon's job is to show us not exactly what He looks like, but ***who He is***. The same can be said for icons of angels. These icons try to show who angels are: bodiless beings reflecting the loving greatness of God, as the moon reflects the light of the sun. If you look very closely at this angel, the Archangel Gabriel, you can see the ends of a dark ribbon flowing out from behind his head. This is a way of showing how Gabriel listens completely to the voice of God. He is bowing his head in humility, and his eyes are brimming with love for the One in whose direction he's always looking. This is what we can learn from the angels: to keep our eyes and hearts on God no matter what we're doing.

NOTICE THIS →

The chips and cracks show that this ancient icon has been through a lot. This adds to its beauty. Like an older person whose face has the wrinkles of experience and endurance, a worn icon teaches us to be strong, peaceful, and faithful to God.

Angel with the Golden Hair

Our Front Gates

If someone ripped up the pictures of the people you love, wouldn't you be upset? Something like this happened to the Church more than a thousand two hundred years ago, when people called iconoclasts began destroying the holy images. During this time lived a pious widow who had an icon so old and beautiful that many thought it had been painted by St. Luke. The widow saved it from the iconoclasts by pushing it out to sea. Amazed, she watched it float away standing upright on the water. Many years later, the monks at the Iveron Monastery on Mount Athos saw the widow's icon coming to them in the same way it had left her, standing on the sea. They set the icon in a special place in their church, but it kept moving mysteriously to the monastery's front gates. Eventually, they got the message that Christ and His mother wanted the icon to guard the entrance. We often think we know the right place for God and want to keep our faith tucked away, but God wants to be out at the "front gates" of our lives.

NOTICE THIS →

See the dried blood on the Theotokos's chin? It's been there for hundreds of years. An attacking pirate stabbed the icon, and blood came gushing out. The pirate then believed in Christ and became an Iveron monk himself.

Original Iveron Icon of the Theotokos

Theodora

Another defender of the icons was Empress Theodora. She understood that we don't pray ***to*** icons; we pray ***through*** them. Wise and patient, she stayed faithful to the truth even though her own husband, the emperor, was an iconoclast. She was quiet, knowing to wait for the right time to raise her voice. So when Theodora became the sole ruler of the Eastern Roman Empire after her husband's death, she demanded that everyone who had been put in jail for honoring the icons be set free. Then she had the leaders of the Church return the icons to their rightful places. Finally, she called for a joyous parade of the holy images. We remember this celebration on the first Sunday of Lent, the Sunday of Orthodoxy. On this day, bishops, priests, monks, nuns, and children all around the world have colorful icon processions like the one St. Theodora called for so long ago.

NOTICE THIS →

Saints' halos show that they shine with Christ's light, that they have drawn close to God and have "caught fire." Iconographers paint the darker colors first, then layer by layer the darkness gives way to light. An icon has no shadows, inviting us to step into the endless day of heaven.

Saint Theodora

Sun-Catchers

Have you ever tried to climb a mountain? It can be hard, but once you reach the top and see the view, you realize it was worth all the work. Imagine how Peter, James, and John felt after Jesus had led them to the top of Mt. Tabor, where He allowed them to see Him through the eyes of heaven. They saw Him shining as God over the mountaintop, like the bright sun rising on a new day. The apostles, letting our Lord's light shine through their whole being, became living sun-catchers. This is why people in icons look different; they've been transformed by God's light, the light of Tabor. The saints remind us to let God transform us every minute of every day so we can become who God created us to be. Sometimes this can seem harder than climbing the highest mountain, but Jesus is not only with us every step of the way; He's waiting for us at the top, reaching out His hand with the words, "Well done, good and faithful servant" (Matthew 25:23).

NOTICE THIS →

Moses and Elijah are heavenly witnesses to Christ's work on earth. Their presence on Mt. Tabor shows that all people, "dead" and alive, are united in Jesus. Icons are windows that allow the light of the next world to shine on us.

The Transfiguration

Rescued Beauty

Sadly, sometimes an icon might get painted over or so damaged that it needs to be repaired before we lose it completely. Once its original appearance has been restored (as happened with the Sinai Christ you saw earlier), an old icon can surprise us with its beauty. This is what it's like with us, who were made in God's image. Jesus came down to restore us, to wipe away the layers of dirt and damage so our original beauty can shine through. Our job is to let Him do His work, as Adam (who represents each one of us) is doing in the icon of the Resurrection. The most powerful thing he can do is to reach out and surrender himself to God's love, to let Christ save him. That's why the icon shows Jesus, in all His bright glory, pulling Adam out of the tomb by his wrist. Without Christ, he would be helpless and lost. So would we.

NOTICE THIS →

Christ's robes are billowing upward because He is going down to rescue everyone. No one stays lost in the darkness. No one is low enough to be beyond His reach. Standing on Hades' broken-down doors, Jesus reassures us that those doors can never again keep anyone prisoner.

The Resurrection

His Lambs

"I am the Good Shepherd; and I know My sheep" (John 10:14). Since the catacombs, we Christians have been comforted by the image of Jesus as the Good Shepherd. We know that no matter how far we may wander, we can never go beyond His reach. He runs to us, lifts us up on His shoulders, and brings us back into the fold. "So will I seek out My sheep; and I will rescue them from all places" (Ezekiel 34:12). In the icon here, the side of Jesus' face that's pressed so tenderly to His lamb looks sad, as if He's saying, "I know what you've been through; I know how scared and alone you felt." Looking at the other side of His face, we can hear comforting words like, "Don't worry; you're in good hands now—the very hands that formed the mountains and seas. These same hands formed you when you were inside your mother. Never forget that you will always be My lamb. I am here to feed you when you're hungry, carry you when you're hurt, find you when you're lost. I am here for you forever."

NOTICE THIS →

Compare this icon to the Sinai Christ. Here, His left hand holds a staff, which, like the Gospel, keeps His sheep on the right path. The right "blessing" hand gently presses the feet of His sheep to His chest, close to His heart.

The Good Shepherd

Defenders of the Icons

So many holy heroes risked life, limb, and freedom, fighting to keep God's image from being violently taken out of the world. Everyone seemed to be against them, but these brave men and women stuck to their faith like paint on wood. They fought valiantly so that we might have the icons and their stories to honor and use as windows of inspiration and doorways to prayer. Here are some facts about a few of the bravest defenders of God's image.

St. Kassiani

BORN: Between 805 and 810 in Constantinople

FEASTDAY: September 7

OCCUPATION: Nun, hymnographer

FAMOUS WORDS: "I hate silence when it is time to speak."

INTERESTING INFO: She was rejected as a potential bride by the future emperor, Theophilos, for being too clever.